3

Earthquakes

by Kathy Furgang

1   Every day an average of fifty earthquakes are detected on Earth's surface. Why do some earthquakes cause major destruction while others go by almost unnoticed? The answer is in the amount of energy they release.

What Causes Earthquakes?

2   An earthquake is a sudden movement or shift of Earth's crust. This thin outer layer is made of many interlocking pieces called tectonic plates. These plates float on a layer of hot molten rock and move as slowly as fingernails grow. As they move, they rub against one another, building up stored energy and pressure. When these plates shift or collide at their boundaries, an earthquake happens. Earth's surface rumbles and shakes as the energy is released.

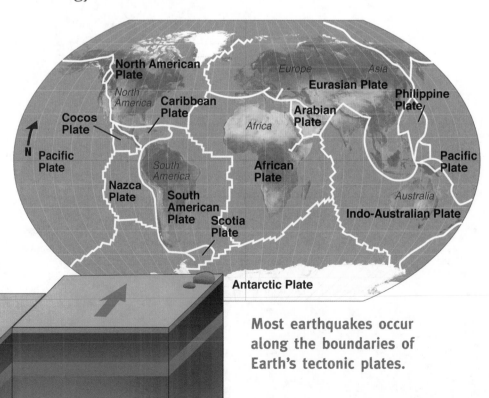

Most earthquakes occur along the boundaries of Earth's tectonic plates.

Measuring Quakes

3   Scientists can measure the strength, or magnitude, of an earthquake with an instrument called a seismograph. In one type of seismograph, seismic waves cause a drum to vibrate as a weighted pen records the vibrations. The longer the lines, the greater the energy released by the quake.

seismograph with drum and pen

Earth's Changing Surface

4   The movement of Earth's tectonic plates reshapes Earth's landscape, building landforms such as mountains and valleys and other land features. As plates move apart, valleys, rivers, and even oceans can form.

5   The Himalayan mountain range in Asia, for example, was formed when the Indo-Australian and Eurasian plates came together. The plates collided and pushed upward, slowly forming the mighty mountain range over the last ten million years.

the Himalayas

Remember to annotate as you read.

Notes

The San Francisco Earthquake, 1906:
An Eyewitness Account

by Emma Burke

At 5:12 a.m. on April 18, 1906, residents of San Francisco, California, were jolted out of their beds by the first shock of a violent earthquake. More than a century later, this quake still ranks as one of the most significant geological events of all time. Emma M. Burke, who lived on Waller Street near Golden Gate Park at the time of the earthquake, published this account of her experiences that fateful day.

1   No one can comprehend the calamity to San Francisco in its entirety. The individual experience can probably give the general public the clearest idea. I was one of the fortunate ones, for neither personal injury nor death visited my household. But what I saw and felt I will try to give to you.

Sacramento Street in San Francisco during the 1906 earthquake

2   It was 5:13 a.m., and my husband had arisen and lit the gas stove, and put on the water to heat. He had closed our bedroom door so that I might enjoy one more nap. We were in a fourth-story apartment flat, said to be built with unusual care.

3   Twelve flats, so constructed, occupied a corner one block from Golden Gate Park. All our rooms, six in number, opened into a square reception hall, from which the stairs descended.

4   The shock came, and hurled my bed against an opposite wall. I sprang up, and, holding firmly to the foot-board managed to keep on my feet to the door. The shock was constantly growing heavier; rumbles, crackling noises, and falling objects already commenced the din.

5   The door refused to open. The earthquake had wedged it in the door-frame. My husband was pushing on the opposite side, and I pulled with all my strength, when a twist of the building released it, and the door sprang open.

6   We braced ourselves in the doorway, clinging to the casing. Our son appeared across the reception room, and my husband motioned to him to stand in his door also, for fear of the chimney.

7   It grew constantly worse, the noise deafening; the crash of dishes, falling pictures, the rattle of the flat tin roof, bookcases being overturned, the piano hurled across the parlor, the groaning and straining of the building itself, broken glass and falling plaster, made such a roar that no one noise could be distinguished.

8   We never knew when the chimney came tearing through; we never knew when a great marine picture weighing one hundred and twenty-five pounds crashed down, not eight feet away from us. We were frequently shaken loose from our hold on the door, and only kept our feet by mutual help and our utmost efforts. The floor moved like short, choppy waves of the sea, crisscrossed by a tide as mighty as themselves. The ceiling responded to all the angles of the floor. I never expected to come out alive. I looked across the reception-room at the white face of our son, and thought to see the floors give way with him momentarily. How a building could stand such motion and keep its frame intact is still a mystery to me.

9   Stand in front of your clock and count off forty-eight seconds, and imagine this scene to have continued for that length of time, and you can get some idea of what one could suffer during that period. . . .

10   My husband told me to dress quickly and get down our tortuous stairs to the street. I rushed to the window and saw my neighbor of the lower flat standing in the middle of the street in her nightclothes, clasping her little babe in her arms. I called to her and asked if I should fling out some bed clothing to wrap them in. She said her husband had gone into the house to get their clothes. The street was black with people, or rather white, for they were mostly in street undress.

11   Then I turned to dress myself. What a change in values! I had no thought for the dress I had cherished the day before. I was merely considering what was warmest and most substantial. A coarse wool skirt, and a long coat lined with white silk and highly decorated with trimming. Did I choose the latter because it was pretty? No, indeed! But because it was warm and long. My diamonds and money were thrust into a hand-satchel, and we hastily made our way to the street. . . .

12   After a half-hour we came up to our flat to take an inventory of the situation. I walked over the remains of my choicest china, porcelain, and cut-glass, without a feeling of regret or a sigh or tear. Everything seemed so insignificant, and the world so far away. That is, the world we had lived in. All estimates of value were annihilated. Human life seemed the only thing worth consideration.

The 1906 earthquake and the fire that followed caused major devastation throughout San Francisco. More than 80 percent of the city was destroyed.

Tsunami!

1   Deep under the ocean, an underwater earthquake disturbs the water. Waves roll out and grow taller as they travel toward land. A tsunami is born!

2   A tsunami can be one huge ocean wave or a series of waves. In the deep ocean, these waves move incredibly fast, traveling hundreds of miles an hour. However, on the surface, the waves appear small and insignificant, so passing ships don't notice them. As they move toward land, they slow down and grow taller and taller. Some waves measure more than 21 meters (70 feet) high!

3   When a tsunami hits land, it can cause unbelievable destruction. People, homes, and trees are picked up and tossed around. Those lucky enough to survive face nearly impossible challenges. Their homes and neighborhoods may have disappeared. Family members and friends may have died.

4   One of the most destructive tsunamis occurred on December 26, 2004. It was set off by a strong underwater earthquake in the Indian Ocean, causing severe damage to more than ten countries in Southern Asia and Eastern Africa. There was no warning system in the Indian Ocean. People were unaware that a tsunami was coming and were unprepared. More than 200,000 people died.

5   Today tsunami-warning systems have been set up in high-risk areas. Satellites can track tsunami waves more accurately than ever before. Radio-operated buoys float in oceans where tsunamis occur. They can detect unusual waves and transmit warnings to land to help reduce loss of life.

BuildReflectWrite

Build Knowledge

Examine the causes and effects of earthquakes. Cite examples from the text to support your responses.

Earthquakes	
Identify some causes of earthquakes.	Evidence:
Explain how earthquakes affect landforms.	Evidence:
Describe how earthquakes affect people.	Evidence:

Reflect

How do Earth's natural processes impact our lives?

Based on this week's texts, write down new ideas and questions you have about the essential question.

_____

_____

_____

_____

_____

_____

Research and Writing

Research an Earth change event in the recent or distant past. Present a fictional, firsthand account of what you saw, heard, and felt during and after the event.

Choose Your Topic

This week, conduct a preliminary search to identify an Earth change event you would like to research. Construct three or more guiding questions that will help you focus your research on the information you will need to present your account.

Remember to annotate as you read.

Notes

Volcanoes

by Brett Kelly

1   At first glance, Naples appears to be like any other bustling European city. Tucked along the west coast of Italy, Naples has a picturesque bay to the west and a majestic mountain rising to the east. Look closer, however, and you will see that the nearby mountain is in fact Mount Vesuvius—a very large, active volcano. When it erupted in 79 CE, it rained poisonous gases, rock, ash, and scalding hot lava down on the surrounding cities and their inhabitants.

2   What causes violent volcanic eruptions like this? The answer lies deep within Earth.

Italy is home to Europe's only active volcano.

Mount Vesuvius erupted most recently in 1944.

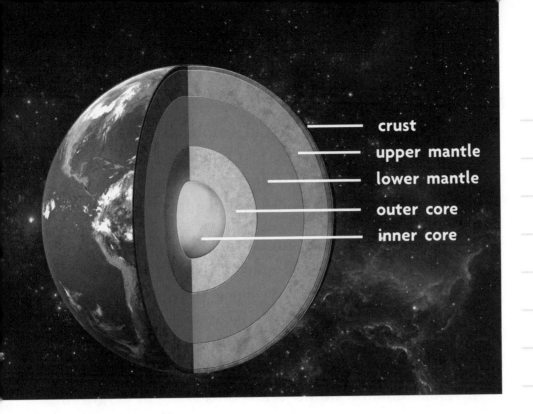

crust
upper mantle
lower mantle
outer core
inner core

Earth's Layers

3   The surface of Earth is always changing because of its structure. Earth is made up of four different layers: the crust, the mantle, the outer core, and the inner core. The crust, or solid outer shell, is the thinnest of the four layers, and it is the one we live on. The crust is formed from giant slabs, or plates, of rock. These plates fit together like pieces of a jigsaw puzzle. Together they float on another layer called the mantle.

4   The mantle is the layer that surrounds Earth's core, or center. It is about 2,900 kilometers (1,800 miles) deep. The mantle is divided into two sections. The upper mantle is composed of cold, dense rock. The lower mantle is made of partially molten rock that flows. This is the area that causes the shifting of the tectonic plates just below Earth's surface, creating volcanoes and earthquakes.

5   The next layer is Earth's outer core, which is made up of very hot liquid (molten) lava. The outer core is about 4,800 kilometers (3,000 miles) beneath the surface of Earth. The inner core is even deeper. It is a solid ball made of metals.

6   The heat and pressure inside Earth are so great that solid rock is constantly melting and forming liquid magma. Because the liquid magma is lighter than solid rock, the magma rises and the solid rock sinks. Some magma cools as it rises, becoming solid rock and sinking again. Other magma remains liquid and collects in underground chambers. When the heat and pressure build in these chambers, the magma is pushed through cracks in Earth's surface. The result is a volcanic eruption. Magma that has erupted through cracks in Earth's crust is called lava.

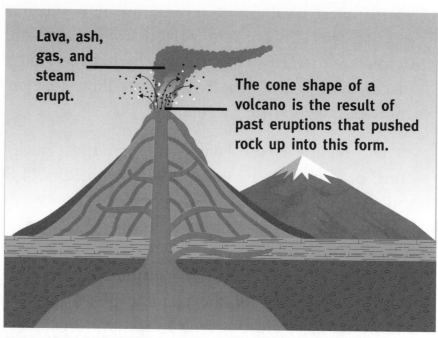

Lava, ash, gas, and steam erupt.

The cone shape of a volcano is the result of past eruptions that pushed rock up into this form.

Hot melted rock, called magma, rises from the magma chamber, making tubes, called pipes, along the way. Some magma goes straight up the volcano and out the top. Some magma escapes through side vents in the volcano.

Plate Boundaries

7   According to the U.S. Geological Survey (USGS), there are seven major plates on Earth, subdivided into smaller plates. As these plates float, they slowly slide past each other, spread apart, or collide. Where two plates meet is called a plate boundary. Most volcanoes occur at plate boundaries. Vesuvius, for example, is part of a line of volcanoes that formed over the boundary between the African and Eurasian plates. Some volcanoes, however, occur at the interior of plates. These spots are thought to be especially hot regions in Earth's mantle that spew magma onto Earth's surface. These areas are called hot spots. Pico do Fogo, for example, sits on the African plate and is therefore considered a hot spot volcano. Hot spots can create entire chains of islands, like those forming the U.S. state of Hawaii.

Pico do Fogo, a hot spot volcano, last erupted in 1995.

8   Volcanoes can be found on land and along the ocean floor. Volcanic eruptions on land can create mountains or form craters that become lakes. Volcanic eruptions underwater may cause a sea or lake to boil. Deep-sea eruptions can also form islands over time.

9   Some volcanoes are dormant, or sleeping. That means they haven't erupted for a long time. Others are extinct and will never erupt again. Volcanoes that are erupting now or have erupted in recent times, such as Vesuvius or Fogo, are referred to as active volcanoes.

10   Today, Earth has about 1,500 active volcanoes on dry land. Another 10,000 volcanoes can be found along the ocean floor.

11   Most volcanic activity happens along the boundary of the Pacific plate. Scientists call this circle beneath the Pacific Ocean the Ring of Fire. It is most active because the Pacific plate is huge. When it collides with other plates, the edges of the other plates buckle and compress. The result is a higher rate of earthquakes and volcanoes.

Crater Lakes

On the island of Flores in Indonesia, a volcano has created three crater lakes that change colors. The lakes can appear green, blue, black, or red, depending on the release of underground gases.

Famous Eruptions

12   The most famous volcanic eruption in history occurred at Mount Vesuvius in Italy in 79 CE. Pompeii and two neighboring towns were wiped out within just a few hours. As many as 16,000 people are believed to have died as their homes were buried under layers of rock and ash. The eruption sealed the region as if in a time capsule for more than 1,700 years. It wasn't until the eighteenth century that archaeologists uncovered the lost cities again. They found people and their pets preserved in volcanic ash in the exact positions they were in when they died. Also preserved were the remains of homes, fountains, and a theater. Even the fresco paintings decorating some walls were preserved. We have learned much more about this ancient time from uncovering Pompeii than we have from other cities that aged normally.

13   Most rocks that erupt from Vesuvius are andesite, a type of volcanic rock that creates explosive eruptions. This makes Vesuvius an especially dangerous and unpredictable volcano. According to a geologist at the Field Museum in Chicago, "When those kinds of volcanoes erupt, they tend to erupt explosively." The huge explosions create columns of gas, ash, and rock that can rise dozens of kilometers into the atmosphere.

14   The kind of eruption that occurred on Mount Vesuvius is described as "Plinian," named for Pliny the Elder, a Roman nobleman who died as a result of the 79 CE volcano eruption. More recently, another Plinian eruption occurred in the Philippines. Mount Pinatubo had not had any major activity for 500 years. But in the spring of 1991, there were minor eruptions and earthquakes. Scientists took these as signs that Mount Pinatubo might erupt. So the government ordered an evacuation of about 66,000 people. Then, on June 15, 1991, Mount Pinatubo did erupt. More than 850 people died. The death toll would have been much higher without the evacuation plan.

Plinian Eruptions

A "Plinian" eruption takes its name from Pliny the Elder, a Roman nobleman and historian who died during the 79 CE eruption of Mount Vesuvius. His nephew, Pliny the Younger, wrote the only surviving description of the blast.

From one of the mountaintops across the bay, Pliny the Younger noticed "a cloud of unusual size and appearance." He compared the cloud's shape to that of a pine tree, "for it rose to a great height on a sort of trunk and then split off into branches." This cloud was actually a poisonous column of gas mixed with thousands of tons of rock and ash blasting out of the volcano's chamber.

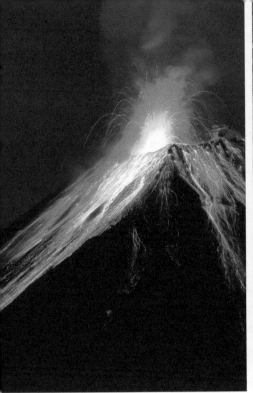

Living in Volcanic Regions

15   When volcanoes do erupt, they can swiftly destroy habitats, towns, and their inhabitants. They can change the landscape, knocking down trees and moving land. They can create avalanches and mudflows, which can be devastating. Eruptions have turned daylight skies to night. Some effects of volcanoes can be far-reaching. Volcanic ash clouds can affect global weather patterns.

16   Scientists will continue to study volcanoes and their effects. In the meantime, cities near some volcanoes are improving their evacuation plans and teaching volcano safety. Some are banning new construction in hazardous areas. New satellite technology allows scientists to monitor and measure plate shifts and volcanic activity from outer space. This could allow scientists to better predict volcanic eruptions in the future.

Notes

Word Study Read

Remember to annotate as you read.

Notes

The Mount St. Helens Volcano

1   Until 1980, Mount St. Helens was a symbol of Washington's natural beauty. Located in the southern part of the state, thousands of people visited the mountain to hike, camp, and picnic. For more than 100 years, the volcano was peaceful.

2   Then on March 20, 1980, several earthquakes rocked the mountain. Many people were surprised. However, geologists who had been studying the volcano for years weren't surprised at all. In 1978, the U.S. Geological Survey, an organization of scientists that includes geologists, ecologists, and archaeologists, published a bulletin. It stated that Mount St. Helens was likely to erupt before the end of the twentieth century.

3   Unfortunately, the scientists turned out to be right. On the morning of May 18, 1980, Mount St. Helens erupted with great force. Clouds of smoke, steam, and ash filled the air. The sky was as dark as night. The eruption continued for hours, destroying 596 square kilometers (230 square miles). Plant and animal habitats on the mountain were disrupted and devastated, and 57 people died.

4   After the disaster, the United States Congress created the Mount St. Helens National Monument. It included an area of 110 acres around Mount St. Helens. It was set aside so that scientists could study the geology and ecology of the land. Over the past decades, life has slowly returned to the land. New forests have grown, and animals have created new habitats. Thanks to the National Monument, scientists have been able to observe and study how life returns on its own after a major eruption.

BuildReflectWrite

Build Knowledge

Record new information you learned this week.

Volcanoes	
Explain what causes volcanoes.	**Explain where volcanoes happen.**
Describe how volcanoes affect landforms, and cite an example from the text.	**Describe how volcanoes affect people, and cite some examples from the text.**

Reflect

How do Earth's natural processes impact our lives?

Based on this week's texts, write down new ideas and questions you have about the essential question.

_____

_____

_____

_____

_____

_____

Research and Writing

Research an Earth change event in the recent or distant past. Present a fictional, firsthand account of what you saw, heard, and felt during and after the event.

Conduct Research

Use your guiding questions to conduct research this week. Gather information from at least three sources, including both print and online sources. Use your sources to plan your fictional, firsthand account.

Notes

Mount Vesuvius, 79 CE:

Letter from Pliny the Younger

On August 24, 79 CE, one of the most powerful volcanoes in the world, called Mount Vesuvius, erupted in southern Italy. Spewing molten ash and rock into the air, it destroyed the city of Pompeii and two other resort towns nearby. People suffocated from the ash and gas that came forth from the eruption. Then volcanic debris literally buried Pompeii and the surrounding area. The cities were forgotten and stayed buried for almost 1,700 years. Excavations began in 1748 and continue today. Amazingly, because the area was buried so quickly by volcanic ash, everything and everyone was well preserved.

A voice from ancient Pompeii reaches us through his written account of the Mount Vesuvius eruption. This writer is named Pliny the Younger, and his letters provide an eyewitness account of the last hours of a Roman city. During the eruption, he was staying in the home of his uncle, Pliny the Elder. The elder Pliny was a renowned scholar and an official in the Roman court and navy.

This excerpt is a translation of the Latin text.

The Eruption of Vesuvius, Johan Christian Dahl, 1826

To Cornelius Tacitus:

1   That letter I wrote to you concerning the death of my uncle has raised your curiosity, it seems. Therefore, I will relay the terrors and dangers. . . .

2   My uncle having left us, I spent such time as was left on my studies, until it was time for my bath. Afterwards, I went to supper and then fell into a short and uneasy sleep. For many days we had noticed a trembling of the earth. This did not alarm us much, as this is quite an ordinary occurrence in Campania. But the quivering earth was especially violent that night. It not only shook, but also overturned everything around us. My mother rushed into my bedroom, where she found me rising to awaken her. We sat down in the open area of the house, in a small space between the buildings and the sea. As I was only eighteen years of age, I don't know whether I should call my behavior, in this dangerous time, courage or folly. But I took up my book, and amused myself with reading, and even making notes, as if I had been perfectly at my leisure.

3   Just then, a Spanish friend of my uncle's joined us. Observing me sitting by my mother with a book in my hand, he scolded her for her calmness, and me for my careless security. Nevertheless, I went on with my book. Though it was now morning, the light was still dim. The buildings all around us tottered. Though we stood upon open ground, there was no remaining ground that was not in danger. We therefore decided to leave our town.

4   A panic-stricken crowd followed us. Because a mind distracted with terror doubts its own decisions, they pressed behind us. We then stood still in front of a most dangerous and dreadful scene. The chariots rocked backwards and forwards, even though they were upon level ground. We could not keep them steady, even by supporting them with large stones. The sea seemed to roll back upon itself. I am certain that the beach was considerably larger. Several sea animals were left stranded upon it. Above, a black and dreadful cloud, broken with rapid, zigzag flashes, revealed behind it variously shaped masses of flame. The bigger flames were like sheet-lightning, but much larger. Upon this our Spanish friend addressed himself to my mother and me with great energy and urgency.

In the nineteenth century, archaeologists discovered the bodies of those who had died in Pompeii when Mount Vesuvius erupted in 79 CE. Their bodies had been preserved by volcanic ash, in exactly the positions they had been in at the time. Archaeologists made plaster casts of those remains, which are on display in Pompeii today.

the ruins of the bakery in Pompeii

5   "If your brother," he said, "if your uncle is safe, he certainly wishes you to be safe too. But if he died, I'm sure it was his desire that you both survive. Why, therefore, do you delay your escape a moment?"

6   We said we could never think of our own safety while we were uncertain of his. Upon this our friend left us, and quite speedily fled from the danger.

7   Soon afterwards, the cloud began to lower and cover the sea. It had already hidden the island of Capri and the promontory of Misenum. My mother now begged, urged, and even commanded me to make my escape. Because I was young, I could easily do that. As for herself, she said her age and weight made the journey impossible. However, she said she would willingly meet death as long as she did not cause mine. But I absolutely refused to leave her. I took her by the hand, and forced her to go with me. She agreed reluctantly, but not without many instances of her scolding herself for slowing my flight.

8   The ashes now began to fall upon us, though at first not in great quantity. I looked back. A dense dark mist seemed to be following us. It spread itself over the country like a cloud.

9   "Let us go up the high-road," I said, "while we can still see. I fear that, should we fall in the road, we will be pressed to death in the dark by the crowds that are following us."

10   We had scarcely sat down when night came upon us. It was not like when the sky is cloudy or when there is no moon. But it was like a room when it is shut up, and all the lights put out. We heard the shrieks of women, the screams of children, and the shouts of men. Some were calling for their children, others for their parents, and others for their husbands and wives. They were trying to recognize each other by the voices that replied. One was crying about his own fate, and another that of his family. Some were wishing to die from the very fear of dying. Some were lifting their hands to the gods.

This portrait of the baker Terentius Neo with his wife was found on the wall of a Pompeii house.

11   There were many who were convinced that there now were no gods at all. They believed that the final endless night, the end of the world, had come upon us. Among these people, there were some who magnified the real dangers with fictitious horrors. I remember some who declared that one part of Misenum had fallen, and that another was on fire. The stories were false, but some people believed them. The sky now grew rather lighter, which we imagined to be an approaching burst of flames. And in truth it was. However, the fire fell at a distance from us. Then again we were immersed in thick darkness. A heavy shower of ashes rained upon us. From time to time, we had to stand up to shake off the ashes or be crushed by the weight of them. We would have been buried in the heap. I might boast that during all of this horror, I let out not a sigh or cry of fear. My attitude had been grounded in that sad but mighty and comforting thought that all mankind were involved in the same destruction. I believed I was dying with the whole world.

Vesuvius in Eruption, Joseph Mallord William Turner, 1817

12   At last the dreadful darkness was scattered bit-by-bit, like a cloud or smoke. The real day returned. Even the sun shone out, though with a pale light like when an eclipse is coming on. Every object that presented itself to our weakened eyes seemed changed. Everything was covered deep with ashes, as if by snow. We returned to Misenum, where we cleaned up as well as we could. We endured an anxious night between hope and fear—with a much larger share of the latter. For the earthquake still continued, while many crazed people ran up and down, increasing everyone's agony with their terrible predictions. Even though we saw the danger, my mother and I had no thoughts of leaving this place until we received news of my uncle.

Farewell,
Pliny the Younger

Pliny the Elder (the uncle) died during the eruption of Mount Vesuvius. Pliny the Younger and his mother, Plinia Marcella, escaped with their lives. Several years afterward, he wrote letters to the Roman senator and historian Cornelius Tacitus about the eruption. These letters were discovered and made public in the sixteenth century.

Remember to annotate as you read.

Notes

Escape from Pompeii

1   It is August 24, 79 CE. Marcus and his father are at their fish stall in the forum, Pompeii's busy marketplace. As usual, they are laughing and talking with shoppers who pause at their stall to purchase fish. They have been working since dawn.

2   Marcus's father gazes affectionately at his son. His beloved wife died years ago when Marcus was a small boy. The two are very close.

3   The marketplace is bustling, much like any other day. Suddenly, around noon, there is a fiery blast from Mount Vesuvius, causing the ground to tremble! A huge, dark cloud forms above the mountain, and the wind blows it toward Pompeii. It is dark as night, and hot ash pours down.

4   "Father, what is happening?" Marcus shouts in fear.

5   "It is a fire blast from the mountain!" replies his father. "We must flee or we will surely perish!"

6   "What about all our fish?" asks Marcus.

7   "Leave everything and come quickly!" says his father, as he removes the cloth from their table and holds it above their heads. They race through the streets as chalky, white ash continues to fall. When they reach the bay, they sit, along with others, waiting and watching. Finally, after two days, Mount Vesuvius stops erupting, but by then Pompeii is buried.

8   "We are fortunate to have survived," says Marcus's father. "We shall travel north and settle in a new city, far from the mountains!"

BuildReflectWrite

Build Knowledge

Identify three descriptive details from Pliny the Younger's account and explain how these details have added to your understanding of volcanoes.

Mount Vesuvius		
Descriptive Detail	**What I Knew Before**	**What I Know Now**
1.		
2.		
3.		

Reflect

How do Earth's natural processes impact our lives?

Based on this week's texts, write down new ideas and questions you have about the essential question.

_____

_____

_____

_____

_____

_____

Research and Writing

Research an Earth change event in the recent or distant past. Present a fictional, firsthand account of what you saw, heard, and felt during and after the event.

Write Your Account

Use your research results to draft, revise, and edit your fictional, firsthand account. Share your account with your peers.

Support for Collaborative Conversation

Discussion Prompts

Express ideas or opinions . . .

When I read _____, it made me think that _____.

Based on the information in _____, my [opinion/idea] is _____.

As I [listened to/read/watched] _____, it occurred to me that _____.

It was important that _____.

Gain the floor . . .

I would like to add a comment. _____.

Excuse me for interrupting, but _____.

That made me think of _____.

Build on a peer's idea or opinion . . .

That's an interesting point. It makes me think _____.

If _____, then maybe _____.

[Name] said _____. That could mean that _____.

Express agreement with a peer's idea . . .

I agree that _____ because _____.

I also feel that _____ because _____.

[Name] made the comment that _____, and I think that is important because _____.

Respectfully express disagreement . . .

I understand your point of view that _____, but in my opinion _____ because _____.

That is an interesting idea, but did you consider the fact that _____?

I do not agree that _____. I think that _____ because _____.

Ask a clarifying question . . .

You said _____. Could you explain what you mean by that?

I don't understand how your evidence supports that inference. Can you say more?

I'm not sure I understand. Are you saying that _____?

Clarify for others . . .

When I said _____, what I meant was that _____.

I reached my conclusion because _____.

Group Roles

Discussion Director:
Your role is to guide the group's discussion and be sure that everyone has a chance to express his or her ideas.

Notetaker:
Your job is to record the group's ideas and important points of discussion.

Summarizer:
In this role, you will restate the group's comments and conclusions.

Presenter:
Your job is to provide an overview of the group's discussion to the class.

Timekeeper:
You will track the time and help to keep your peers on task.

Making Meaning with Words

Word	My Definition	My Sentence
boundary (p. 15)		
collided (p. 5)		
destruction (p. 4)		
elder (p. 22)		
global (p. 19)		
revealed (p. 25)		
scalding (p. 12)		
structure (p. 13)		
trembling (p. 24)		
vibrations (p. 5)		

Lexile 760L–1030L

Build Knowledge Across 10 Topic Strands

Government and Citizenship

Character

Life Science

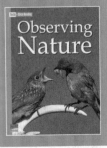

Point of View

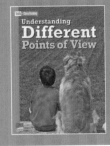

Technology and Society

Theme

History and Culture

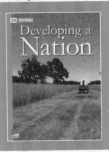

Earth Science

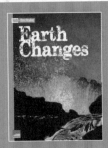

Economics

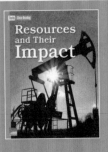

Physical Science

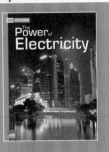

BENCHMARK EDUCATION COMPANY

Grade 4 • Unit 8

ISBN 978-1-4900-9204-1

9 781490 092041